WORLD HISTORY & CULTURES

The Conquistadors

by
Wendy Frey

Don Johnston Incorporated
Volo, Illinois

Edited by:

John Bergez
Start-to-Finish Core Content Series Editor, Pacifica, California

Barbara Armentrout, MA
Start-to-Finish Core Content Developmental Editor, San Carlos, California

Gail Portnuff Venable, MS, CCC-SLP
Speech/Language Pathologist, San Francisco, California

Dorothy Tyack, MA
Learning Disabilities Specialist, San Francisco, California

Jerry Stemach, MS, CCC-SLP
Speech/Language Pathologist, Director of Content Development, Sonoma County, California

Graphics and Illustrations:

Photographs and illustrations are all created professionally and modified to provide the best possible support for the intended reader.
Page 5, 37: The Granger Collection, New York
Page 11: © Brooklyn Museum/Corbis
Page 14: © Stapleton Collection/Corbis
Page 18: © Charles & Josette Lenars/Corbis
Page 19: Courtesy of Eon Images
Page 21: © The Art Archive/Corbis
Page 24 and back cover: Courtesy of the Library of Congress, Hispanic Reading Room
Page 28: Courtesy of the Library of Congress, Prints and Photographs Division [LC-USZ62-37993]
Page 29: Courtesy of the Library of Congress, Prints and Photographs Division [LC-USZ62-102038]
Page 30 and back cover: Courtesy of the National Park Service
Page 39: © 2006 JupiterImages Corporation
All other photos not credited here or with the photo are © Don Johnston Incorporated and its licensors.

Narration:

Professional actors and actresses read the text to build excitement and to model research-based elements of fluency: intonation, stress, prosody, phrase groupings and rate. The rate has been set to maximize comprehension for the reader.

Published by:

Don Johnston Incorporated
26799 West Commerce Drive
Volo, IL 60073

800.999.4660 USA Canada
800.889.5242 Technical Support
www.donjohnston.com

International Standard Book Number
ISBN 978-1-4105-0921-5

Table of Contents

Introduction: A Meeting of Two Worlds

In 1532, two men met in the Andes, the high mountains of Peru, where the Incas lived. One man was an Inca ruler named Atahualpa. The other man was a Spanish explorer named Francisco Pizarro.

Atahualpa was seated on a golden throne. Each time he moved, the gold and silver decoration in his clothing caught the light. To the thousands of Inca soldiers who surrounded him, he seemed to shimmer like the sun.

Pizarro sat stiffly on his horse. He was frightened by the sight of the Inca soldiers, but he did not show his fear. His men hid their fear, too.

An Inca drew this picture of Pizarro meeting Atahualpa. The man in the brown robe is a Spanish priest.

When the two men met, Pizarro was thousands of miles from any Spanish settlement, in a place he had never been before. He had fewer than 200 soldiers with him. Atahualpa was in the middle of his own lands with an army of over 30,000 men.

What do you think happened next? The answer may surprise you.

Pizarro captured Atahualpa within a few hours of meeting him. And within a few months, Pizarro was in control of all the Inca lands. In the first chapter, you will learn how he did this.

Pizarro was just one of the Spanish explorers who went to the **Americas** in the 1500s. The Americas include North America, South America, and the Caribbean Islands. The explorers were following the route of Christopher Columbus, who had sailed there in 1492. They had heard Columbus's stories of land and gold just waiting to be found. Many young Spanish men sailed across the ocean in search of wealth and adventure. In this book, you will discover what happened when the Spanish came to the Americas, which they called the **New World**. You will learn how the Spanish and the people of the New World changed each other's lives.

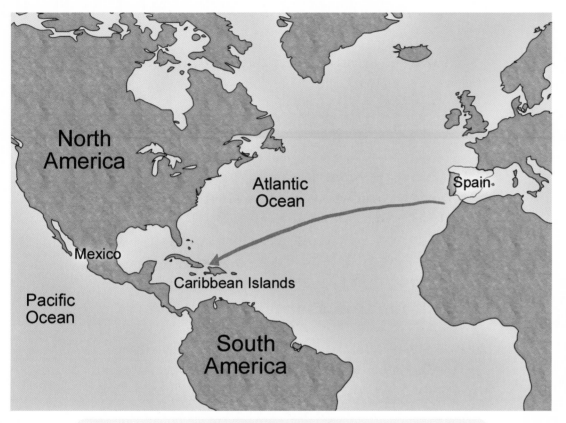

The red arrow shows Christopher Columbus's route from Spain to the Caribbean Islands in the New World.

Chapter One

Pizarro and Atahualpa

Questions this chapter will answer:

- **Why did Pizarro go to Peru?**

- **Who was Atahualpa?**

- **How did Pizarro capture Atahualpa?**

- **How did Pizarro take over the Inca Empire?**

The meeting between Atahualpa and Pizarro was important because it was a meeting of people from two very different worlds. What brought Pizarro to Peru? What was Atahualpa like? And how did the small group of Spanish soldiers defeat the huge Inca army? In this chapter, you will learn how the Incas lost their empire to Spain.

Pizarro: Looking for Gold and Land

At the start of the 1500s, the rulers of Spain wanted to make Spain the most powerful country in Europe. They tried to do this by conquering (taking over) new lands.

Spanish kings encouraged men to go to the New World and to take as much land and gold as they could find. The explorers would have to give most of it to Spain, but they could keep some for themselves.

The explorers were also trained soldiers, so they were ready to fight for any treasures they found. The Spanish called these men **conquistadors**.

Of course, there were millions of people already living in the New World. You might think the land and gold belonged to them. But the conquistadors thought they had the right to take what they could from these native people.

Francisco Pizarro

Francisco Pizarro was a conquistador. In 1502, he went to the New World, where he soon became rich and powerful.

Then Pizarro heard about the rich Inca Empire in the land we now call Peru. Pizarro was eager to find more gold and to take the Incas' lands for Spain. So he decided to lead an **expedition** to Peru. An expedition is a group of people making a trip for a special purpose.

The red arrow shows Pizarro's route into the land of the Incas.

Atahualpa: Ruler of a Huge Empire

At the time the Spanish came to Peru, the Incas had the largest **empire** in the Americas. If a country or a group has an empire, this means that it has power over other groups or countries. The Incas controlled more land than any other group in the Americas. The Inca Empire spread out over 2500 miles from north to south in the Andes Mountains. This area includes some of the highest mountains in the world.

The emperor (ruler) of this huge empire was Atahualpa. The Incas believed that Atahualpa was related to the god of the sun. He had complete power over his people. They were not even allowed to look him in the eye. Everything in the empire belonged to him. All his palaces glittered with gold decoration. He even had a garden that had tiny pieces of gold for dirt. In this garden were gold sculptures that were made to look like corn.

Atahualpa

11

This was one of the cities of the Incas, high in the Andes Mountains.

It was not easy to rule an empire as big as this one. One problem was that it was hard to communicate over such a huge mountainous area. But Atahualpa managed to receive regular reports from all over his empire. He was able to do this because the Incas had built over 10,000 miles of roads connecting every part of the empire. There were stairs, rope bridges, and tunnels that went up, down, across, and through the mountains. Runners used these roads to carry messages to Atahualpa.

The Incas did not have a written language. So they sent messages using a system of knots tied in strings. The strings were passed from one runner to the next, the way Olympic athletes pass a stick during a relay race.

Pizarro Captures Atahualpa

From the time the Spanish arrived in Peru, Atahualpa had been getting reports from his runners about the Spanish explorers. He believed that it would not take much to defeat such a small group of men, and he was curious to meet them.

Surrounded by his great army, Atahualpa met Pizarro and his soldiers briefly outside an Inca town. This is the meeting you read about at the beginning of the book. Atahualpa told the Spanish to meet him in the center of town, where he would give them a proper welcome. The Incas were expecting a peaceful meeting, but that was not what the Spanish had in mind.

When the Spanish arrived in the center of town, they quickly hid themselves. Then Atahualpa arrived with only a few thousand guards, and the Spanish leaped out in a surprise attack.

The Incas fought hard, but their weapons were no match for those of the Spanish. Spanish guns killed Inca warriors before they had a chance to get their bows and arrows ready. And the iron swords of the Spanish sliced right through the Incas' wooden spears.

Very quickly, the Spanish killed thousands of Inca warriors and took Atahualpa prisoner.

Pizarro captures Atahualpa.

Pizarro Tricks the Incas

After Pizarro had captured Atahualpa,
he demanded a ransom from the Incas. Ransom
is money that is paid to free a person who has
been captured or kidnapped. Pizarro told the
Incas that he would let Atahualpa go free if
they would give him enough gold and silver
to fill a large room.

This is the tomb of one of Atahualpa's ancestors.
All the decorations are made of gold.

15

To save their ruler, the Inca people took all of the golden treasures out of their temples and sent them to Pizarro. The Spanish quickly melted the treasures and turned them into bricks of gold. The Incas were amazed by how much the Spanish wanted gold. One Inca noble asked them, "Do you eat gold?"

Pizarro went back on his promise. He kept Atahualpa prisoner for eight months, even though the Incas had paid the ransom. Then he killed Atahualpa instead of returning him to his people.

The Inca Empire soon fell apart without its leader. In a few years, the mighty empire was gone, and the Spanish controlled Peru.

Chapter Summary

In this chapter, you learned how Francisco Pizarro conquered the Inca Empire with fewer than 200 soldiers. Pizarro came to Peru looking for gold and land. There, he met Atahualpa, the ruler of the huge Inca Empire. The Spanish were able to capture Atahualpa because they had better weapons than the Incas. Pizarro promised to trade Atahualpa for a roomful of gold, but he went back on his promise and killed Atahualpa.

In the next chapter, you will meet a conquistador named Hernán Cortés and find out what happened when he went to Mexico.

Chapter Two

Cortés and Montezuma

Questions this chapter will answer:

- **What big risk did Cortés take in Mexico?**

- **What difficult decision did the Aztec emperor Montezuma face?**

- **Why did Montezuma welcome the Spanish?**

- **How did Cortés defeat the Aztecs?**

After weeks of walking across the mountains of Mexico, Hernán Cortés and his small band of Spanish soldiers came out on a ridge above a great valley. In the clear mountain air, they could see for miles.

Imagine how surprised Cortés and his men must have been when they saw a huge city below them. It was the biggest city they had ever seen. The city was built on an island in the middle of a glittering lake. At the center of the city, there were great stone pyramids with temples on top of them. One pyramid was more than 100 feet tall.

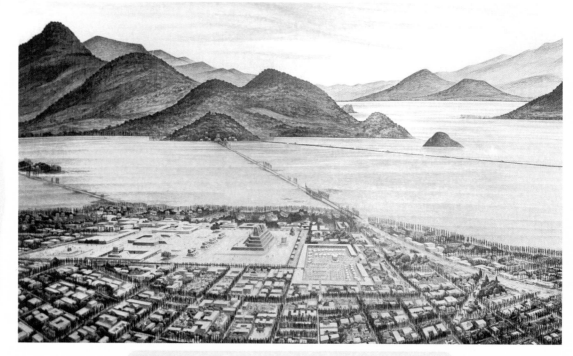

This is the city that Cortés and his men saw.

The Spanish were looking at the capital city of the Aztecs. It was called Tenochtitlán, and it was the home of the emperor Montezuma.

In this chapter, you will discover what Cortés did to reach this amazing city and what happened when he got there.

Cortés Takes a Risk

In Spain, Hernán Cortés dreamed about finding excitement and riches in the New World. At the age of 22, he sailed for Cuba. He became rich very quickly in Cuba, but that was not enough for him. He wanted fame as well. So, in 1519, Cortés decided to lead an expedition to Mexico. He dreamed of finding gold and silver and then returning to Spain in triumph. In February, he set off from Cuba with 11 ships and 530 men.

Hernán Cortés

When he got to Mexico, Cortés had a problem. He wanted to take his men inland to Tenochtitlán, but the city was 200 miles away over the mountains. Cortés was afraid that his men would not want to make the long and difficult trip.

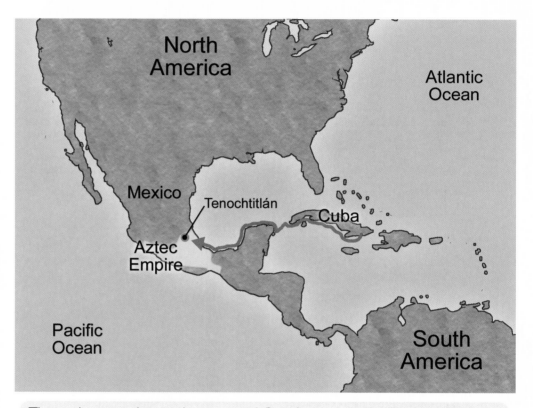

The red arrow shows the route of Cortés into the land of the Aztecs.

Cortés decided to take a big gamble. He took all the supplies off his ships. Then he sank his ships. Now the Spanish would not be able to leave Mexico quickly even if they wanted to. For Cortés, there was no turning back.

Montezuma's Difficult Decision

In 1519, most of the land that is now Mexico was part of the Aztec Empire. The Aztecs had built their empire by defeating their neighbors in war.

When the Spanish arrived in Mexico, the news soon reached the Aztec emperor, Montezuma, at his royal palace in Tenochtitlán. Now Montezuma faced a difficult decision. Should he welcome the strangers to his land, or make war against them?

Like all Aztecs, Montezuma worshipped many gods. An Aztec legend (story) said that one of these gods had sailed away many years before and would return as a white-skinned man with a beard. The legend even said that 1519 was the year when he would return.

Montezuma

Montezuma thought that the leader of these white-skinned men with beards could be this god. If Cortés and his soldiers were men, the Aztecs could fight them. But if they were gods, they must be welcomed.

21

Montezuma Welcomes Cortés

Montezuma decided to treat the Spanish with great honor instead of fighting them. He met Cortés in his royal palace. Montezuma was dressed in his finest clothes, including a cloak covered with feathers of many colors. He welcomed the Spanish and gave them rooms in one of his palaces.

Cortés and his men stayed in a palace like this one.

Cortés behaved in a friendly way at first, and for a few days things seemed to be going well between the Spanish and the Aztecs. But not for long.

The Spanish were shocked when they learned that the Aztecs believed in **human sacrifice**. The Aztecs believed that their sun god made the sun rise each day. To make sure the sun would continue to rise, the Aztecs thought they had to offer the sun god a regular supply of fresh human hearts. To do this, they captured prisoners and cut out the prisoners' hearts while they were still alive.

The Aztecs were not happy with the Spanish either. The Spanish guns and horses frightened them. And the Aztecs were upset when the Spanish took over the main Aztec temple and used it as a Spanish church.

Cortés Defeats the Aztecs

In November 1519, Cortés stopped pretending to be a friend of the Aztecs. He took Montezuma prisoner and kept him in the rooms where the Spanish were living. For several months, Cortés ruled the Aztecs easily by making Montezuma tell his people what the Spanish wanted them to do.

Then, in June 1520, some Spanish soldiers attacked a group of Aztecs during a religious festival. This time the Aztecs fought back. Cortés brought Montezuma up to the roof of the palace where the Spanish were staying, so that Montezuma could ask the Aztecs to be peaceful. But the Aztecs blamed Montezuma for their troubles. They threw stones and shot arrows at him. He was wounded and died. A few days later, the Aztecs forced the Spanish to leave the city.

An Aztec drew this picture of a battle between the Spanish and the Aztecs.

In January 1521, the Spanish returned, and there was a long battle. The Spanish did not have to fight the Aztecs by themselves. Many neighboring groups hated the Aztecs because the Aztecs had conquered them. These groups joined the Spanish to fight the Aztecs.

Seven months later, the Spanish army captured the city of Tenochtitlán. Now, with the capital city in the hands of the Spanish and the emperor dead, the Aztec Empire was finished.

Chapter Summary

In this chapter, you learned what happened when Hernán Cortés went to Mexico. Cortés took a big risk by sinking his ships so that his soldiers would have to follow him to the Aztec capital city. Montezuma, the Aztec emperor, had to decide whether to fight Cortés. Instead he decided to greet Cortés as if he were an Aztec god. But soon Cortés took Montezuma prisoner and defeated the Aztecs with the help of the Aztecs' enemies.

In the next chapter, you will meet a conquistador who is famous for the important places he discovered.

Chapter Three

Coronado's Search for the Cities of Gold

Questions this chapter will answer:

- **Why did Coronado plan a great expedition?**

- **Coronado expected to find a city of gold in the desert. What did he find instead?**

- **What two natural wonders did Coronado discover?**

In the 1500s, there were many legends about the amazing wealth that was waiting to be found in the New World. One of the most interesting legends was the story of the Seven Cities of Gold.

According to this story, there was a great empire called Cíbola that was north of Mexico. Cíbola was said to have seven great cities — each of them filled with gold!

In 1540, a conquistador named Francisco Coronado set out to find the Seven Cities of Gold. In this chapter, you will read about Coronado's adventure and the discoveries he made.

A Grand Expedition

In 1535, Coronado came to Mexico as an assistant to the Spanish governor. It was an important job, but Coronado did not keep it for long.

In 1539, more and more people were hearing about the legend of the Seven Cities of Gold. In that year, a Spanish priest named Father Marcos returned to Mexico from his travels in the north. He said that he had seen one of the golden cities of Cíbola off in the distance.

The Spanish governor was excited about Father Marcos's story. The governor decided to send an expedition to find Cíbola. He asked Coronado to lead the expedition.

Coronado immediately began to plan a grand expedition, much larger than the small expeditions of Cortés and Pizarro. Coronado would lead 230 Spanish horsemen and 62 Spanish foot soldiers. The expedition would also take a lot of supplies and animals, including cattle, goats, and sheep, and 1000 horses. In addition, 600 native Mexicans would come along to help the Spanish. And Father Marcos agreed to go with them as a guide.

Disappointment in the Desert

In February 1540, the expedition headed north. In June, they entered a desert in what is now the state of New Mexico in the United States.

Francisco Coronado leading his expedition across the desert

The expedition was starting to run into trouble. The food supplies were running out, and the tired men were starting to complain. Also, Coronado was starting to wonder about Father Marcos.

The landmarks that Father Marcos said he remembered were never where he said they would be.

But the expedition pushed on. Eventually, it reached the place where Father Marcos said he had seen one of the cities of Cíbola. As Coronado looked out across the valley, he was disappointed. There was no city of gold. Instead, he saw only a small village, with houses made of mud-brick and stone. Today we call this kind of village a **pueblo**.

The name of the village was Hawikuh. It was a village of the Zuni people. The Zuni were fierce warriors. At first, they tried to fight the Spanish. But they soon gave up.

Coronado had been successful in defeating the Zuni, but he felt like a failure because he had not found gold.

A Zuni pueblo

Two Natural Wonders

Coronado was disappointed, but he did not give up. He made the Zuni village his home base and sent out smaller expeditions to see what lay beyond it.

The first expedition went northwest into what is now northern Arizona. The Spanish wanted to see a great river that the Zuni had told them about. After several days, they came to the edge of a huge valley made of rock. The river was at the bottom of the valley, hundreds of feet below them. The Spanish had reached the edge of the Grand Canyon, one of Earth's great natural wonders.

The Grand Canyon

30

The next spring, Coronado led another small group of men into what is now the state of Texas. There, the Spanish found land that was different from anything they had ever seen. It looked as if the land was covered with an endless sea of grass. The men were traveling in the area we now call the Great Plains. In later years, settlers would find out that the Great Plains were very good for farming.

Soon the Spanish saw an even more amazing sight — huge herds of strange animals with humps on their backs. Coronado's men were the first Europeans to describe this animal — the American buffalo.

An American buffalo

31

In the spring of 1542, Coronado decided
to return to Mexico. He had been exploring for
two years, including trips through lands that
are now the states of Oklahoma and Kansas.
And yet he felt he had nothing to show for his
travels. When he died 12 years later, he thought
of himself as a failure.

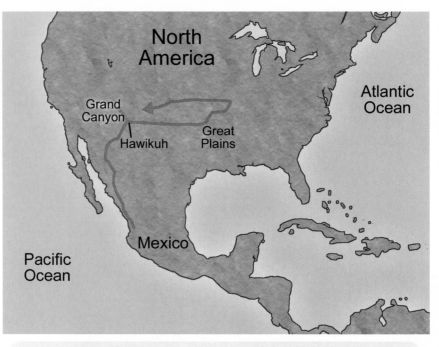

The red arrow shows the route of Coronado's expedition
to look for the Seven Cities of Gold.

It is true that Coronado never found the
gold and silver he was looking for. But he did
find two natural treasures — the Grand Canyon
and the Great Plains. And his travels opened the
way for settlers who would later start farms and
ranches in many of the places he had explored.

Chapter Summary

In this chapter, you learned about Francisco Coronado, who led a large expedition to look for the Seven Cities of Gold. In the desert, Coronado was disappointed to find a little pueblo instead of a great city made of gold. Later he discovered the Grand Canyon and the Great Plains. In the next chapter, you will learn how Coronado and the other conquistadors changed the world.

Chapter Four

How the Conquistadors Changed the World

Questions this chapter will answer:

- **What did the Spanish gain by coming to the Americas?**

- **Why did millions of native people die after the Spanish arrived in the New World?**

- **What happened to the Aztec and Inca cultures?**

After the Spanish defeated the Aztecs at Tenochtitlán, an Aztec poet described his city — and his sadness — this way:

Broken spears lie in the road,

we have torn our hair in grief.

The houses are roofless now,

and their walls are red with blood.

The meeting of the Spanish and the native people in the New World led to huge changes for both groups. The Spanish gained new riches, new foods, and new lands. But for people like the Aztecs and the Incas, the coming of the Spanish was a disaster. In this chapter, you will learn about the different ways the Spanish and the native people of the Americas changed each other's lives.

What the Spanish Got from the Americas

The Spanish gained many important things from the Americas. First, they gained riches. The conquistadors took huge amounts of gold and silver from the Aztec and Inca empires, and sent most of it back to Spain. Because of this, during the 1500s, Spain became one of the richest countries in the world.

Second, the Spanish learned about new foods from the native people in the New World. They learned about **crops** like corn and potatoes. They also learned about a delicious food from the Incas — chocolate.

And finally, the Spanish gained new lands. In years to come, millions of Europeans would follow in the footsteps of the conquistadors and make new lives for themselves in the Americas.

Potatoes are still an important crop in Peru.

How Millions of Native People Died

After the Spanish arrived in the Americas, millions of native people died. Some died in battles with the Spanish. But the greatest number of native people died from diseases that the Spanish brought with them.

One of the diseases that the Spanish brought with them was smallpox. Smallpox was a terrible disease. People who got smallpox had high fevers and sores all over their bodies.

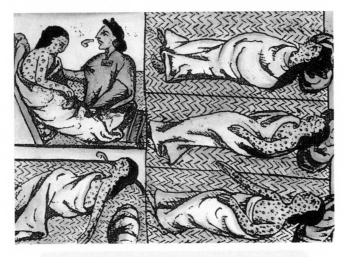

An Aztec drew this picture of people who were sick with smallpox.

European diseases, like smallpox and measles, were new to the people of the Americas. Their bodies had no way to fight the diseases, so the diseases killed them.

The European diseases killed millions of people in the Americas. When the Spanish arrived in Mexico in 1519, about 20 million people were living there. In 1618, there were fewer than two million people.

What Happened to Native Cultures

The diseases that killed the native people helped the Spanish conquer the Aztec and Inca empires. The Spanish then turned these lands into their own empire.

As they built their own empire, the Spanish destroyed much of the culture of the Aztecs and the Incas. They took statues, masks, and jewelry and melted these beautiful objects down to turn them into bars of gold. They tore down temples and palaces, and used the stones to build their own cities. Today, very few buildings remain from these great empires.

This is where the great temple of the Aztecs once stood.

The Spanish also worked hard to get the native people to become Christians. After the Aztecs and Incas were defeated, many Spanish **missionaries** came to the Americas. Missionaries are people who are sent out by a church to spread its ideas. Spanish missionaries built many churches in the Americas. They convinced thousands of natives to become Christians.

But the Aztec and Inca cultures did not disappear completely. The Inca language is still spoken every day in Peru. Many Inca women still weave cloth with patterns that their ancestors used. On special festival days, the grandchildren of the Aztecs perform the dances of their ancestors and play their ancestors' music on drums and flutes.

The man in the photo on the left is doing an Aztec dance. The people in the photo on the right are wearing clothes with Inca patterns.

Chapter Summary

In this chapter, you learned about the different ways the Spanish and the native people of the Americas changed each other's lives. The Spanish gained riches, new foods, and lands by coming to the Americas, but millions of native people died after the Spanish arrived. Most of them were killed by diseases the Spanish brought to the Americas. Much of the culture of the Aztecs and Incas was destroyed, but some parts of those cultures can still be seen today.

Glossary

Word	Definition	Page
Americas	North America (which includes Mexico), South America, and the Caribbean Islands	6
conquistadors	men who came from Spain to the **New World** to take land and gold for Spain *Conquistador* means "conqueror" in Spanish.	9
crops	plants that people grow in large amounts to eat, such as corn and potatoes	36
empire	a group of lands or countries controlled by one powerful group or country	11
expedition	a group of people making a trip for a special purpose	10
human sacrifice	killing people as an offering to the gods	23

Word	Definition	Page
missionary	a person who is sent by a church to spread its ideas	39
New World	the name that the Europeans used for the **Americas**	6
pueblo	a village of the native people of Arizona or New Mexico	29

About the Author

Wendy Frey grew up in New York City, and went to college in Iowa. One of Wendy's first jobs was working as an editor on a radio show. Then, she decided she wanted to write books, so she went back to college to study writing. Since then, she has written history books for young people. She also writes poetry and is working on a novel.

Wendy is interested in painting, photography, sculpture, and travel. She has visited Asia, Europe, Africa, and Central America.

About the Narrator

Andrew Shapiro was born and raised in Virginia. Now he lives and works in Chicago. He has been a voice actor and TV actor for many years. You may have even seen him on TV playing one of the bad guys in *America's Most Wanted*. Andrew likes to travel, play video games, and ride his motorcycle, even in the winter.

A Note to the Teacher

Start-to-Finish Core Content books are designed to help students achieve success in reading to learn. From the provocative cover question to the carefully structured and considerate text, these books promote inquiry, active engagement, and understanding. Not only do students learn curriculum-relevant content, but they learn how to read with understanding. Here are some of the features that make these books such powerful aids in teaching and learning.

Structure That Supports Inquiry and Understanding

Core Content books are carefully structured to encourage students to ask questions, identify main ideas, and understand how ideas relate to one another. The structural features of the Blue Core Content books include the following:

- **"Introduction"**: A concise introduction engages students in the book's topic and explicitly states the book's themes.
- **Clearly focused chapters:** Each of the following chapters focuses on a single topic at a length that makes for a comfortable session of reading.
- **"Questions This Chapter Will Answer"**: Provocative questions following the chapter title reflect the chapter's main ideas. Each question corresponds to a heading within the chapter.
- **Chapter introduction:** An engaging opening leads to a clear statement of the chapter topic.
- **Carefully worded headings:** The headings within each chapter are carefully worded to signal the main idea of the section and reflect the opening questions.
- **Clear topic statements:** Within each chapter section, the main idea is explicitly stated so that students can distinguish it from supporting details.
- **"Chapter Summary"**: A brief summary recaptures the main ideas signaled by the opening questions, text headings, and topic statements.

Text That Is Written for Success™

Every page of a Core Content book is the product of a skilled team of educators, writers, and editors who understand your students' needs. The text features of these books include the following:

- **Mature treatment of grade level curriculum:** Core Content is age and grade-appropriate for the older student who is actively acquiring reading skills. The books also contain information that may be new to any student in the class, empowering Core Content readers to contribute interesting information to class discussions.
- **Idioms and vocabulary:** The text limits the density of new vocabulary and carefully introduces new words, new meanings of familiar words, and idioms. New subject-specific terms are bold-faced and included in the Glossary.
- **Background knowledge:** The text assumes little prior knowledge and anchors the reader using familiar examples and analogies.
- **Sentence structure:** Blue level text introduces a greater variety of complex sentences than are used at the easier Gold level to help students make a transition to the language of traditional textbooks.

For More Information

To find out more about Start-to-Finish Core Content, visit www.donjohnston.com for full product information, standards and research base.